FLIPPING

zombies

www.flippingzombies.co.uk

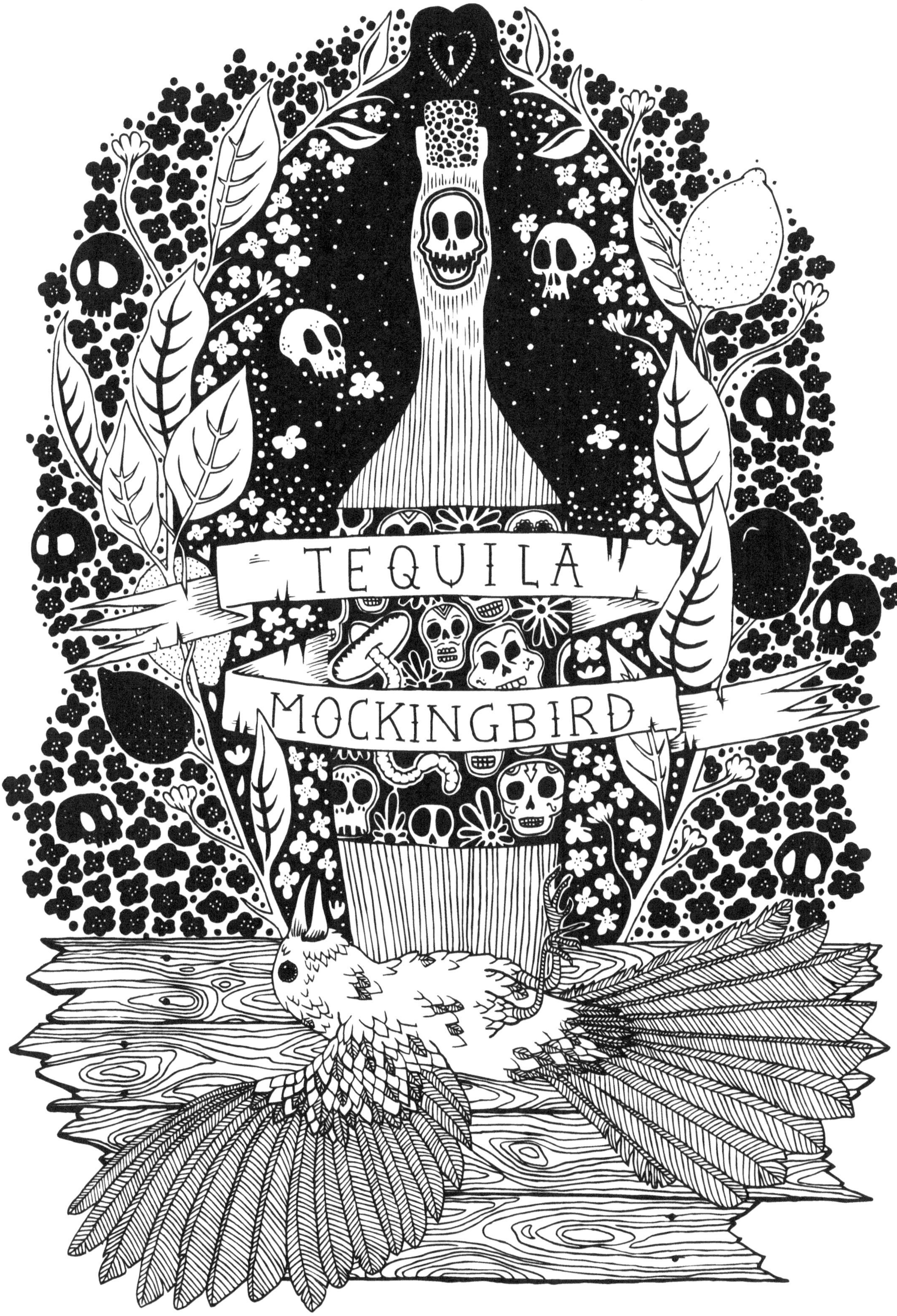
TEQUILA
MOCKINGBIRD

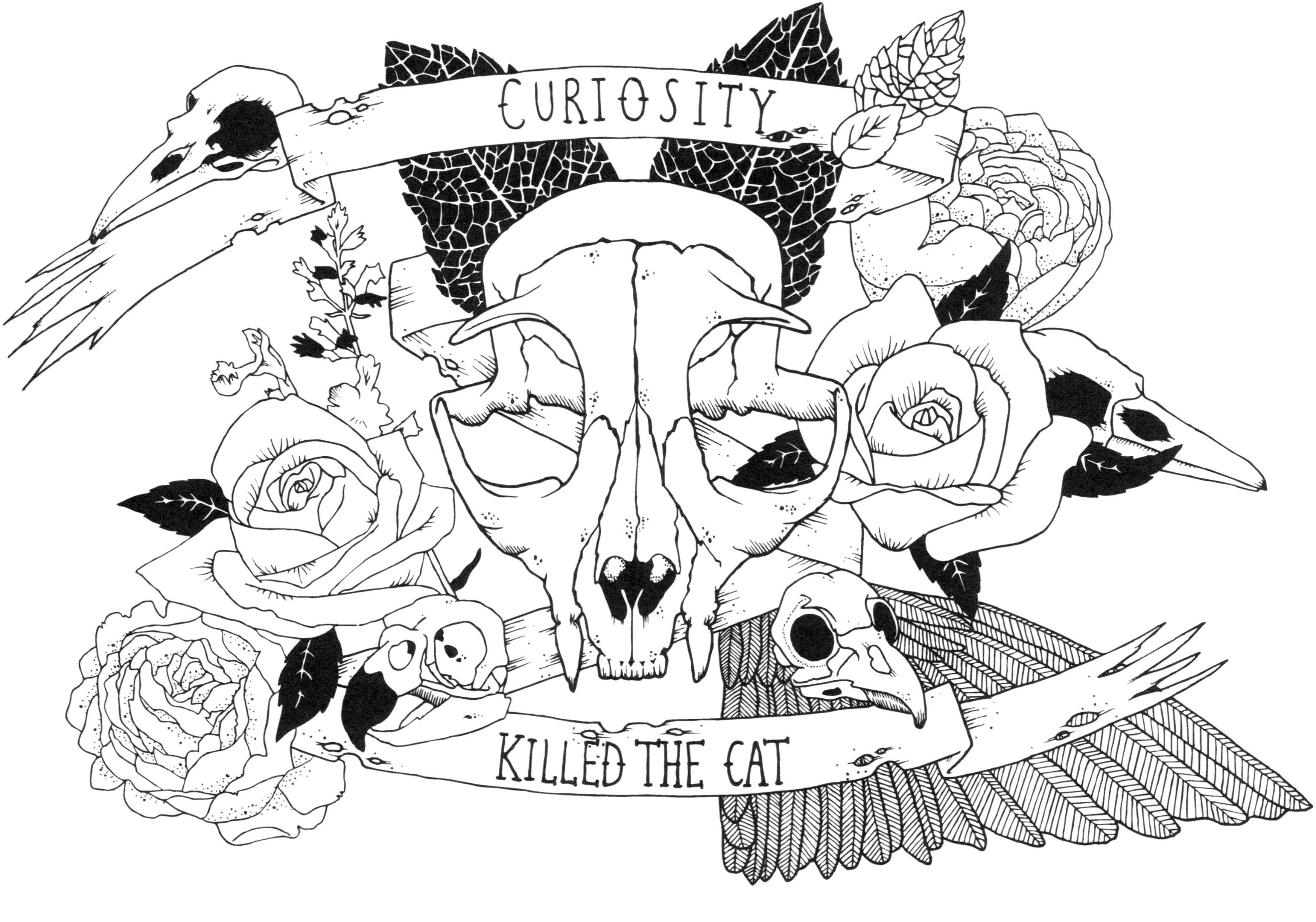
CURIOSITY
KILLED THE CAT

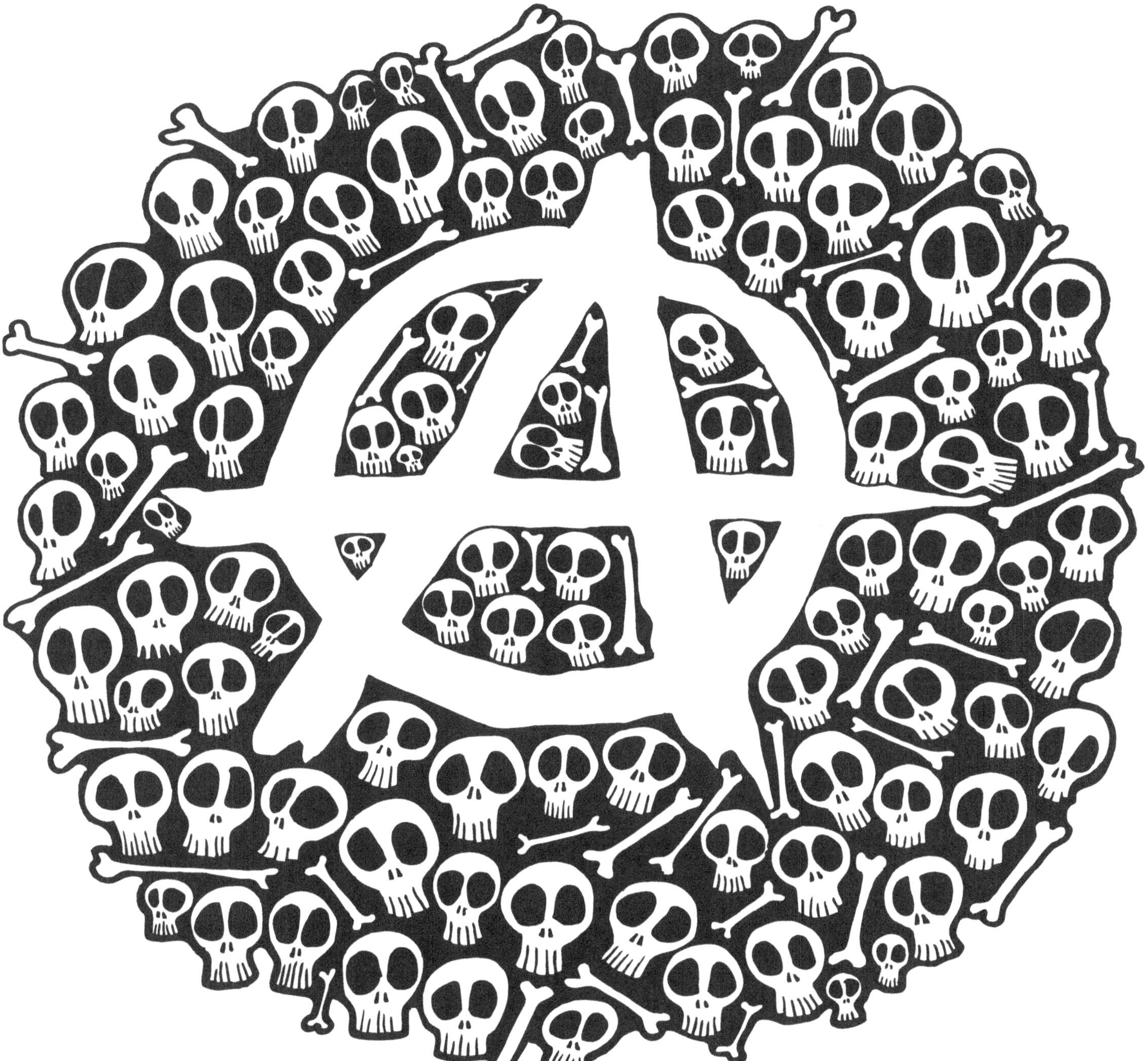

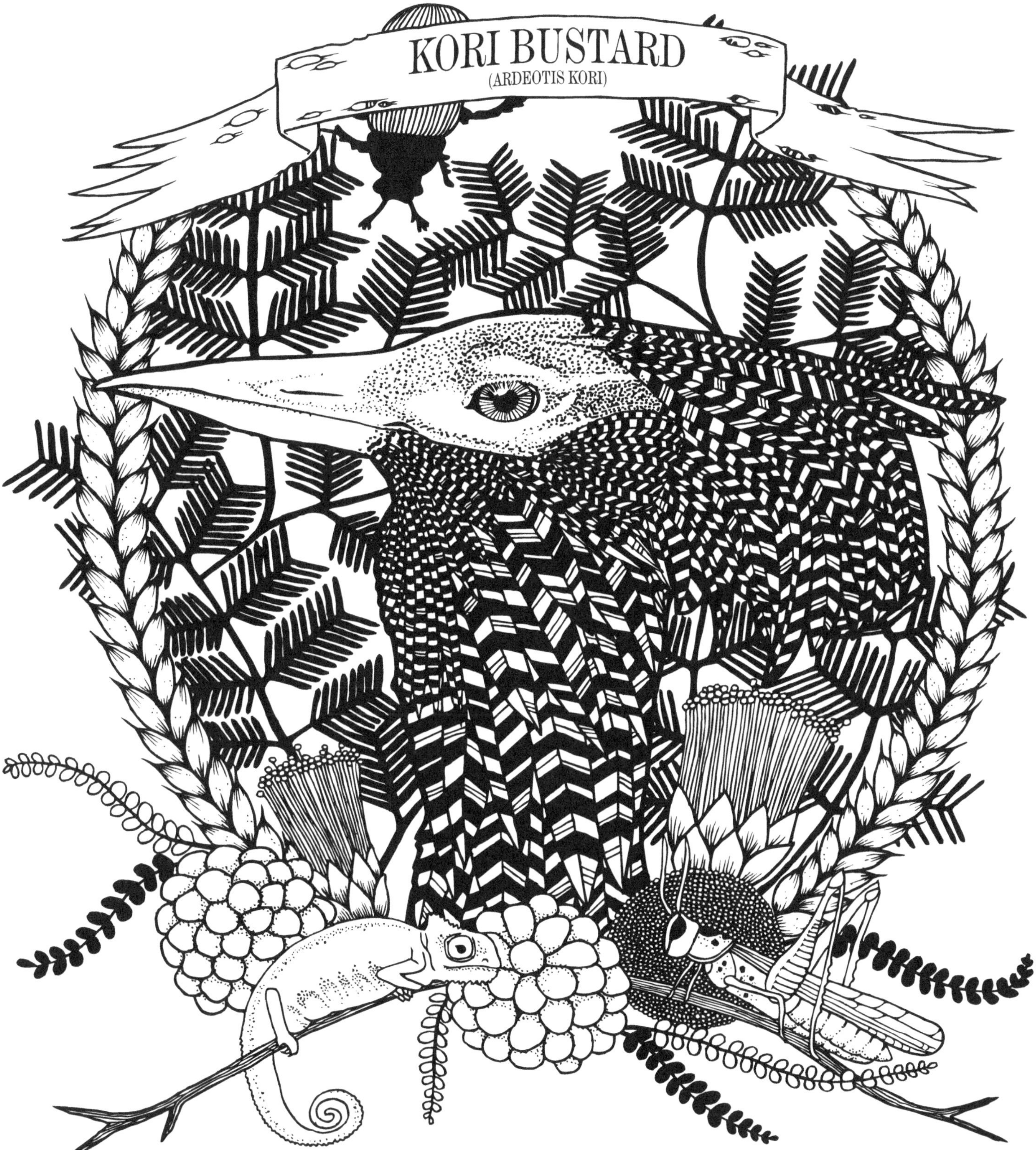
KORI BUSTARD
(ARDEOTIS KORI)

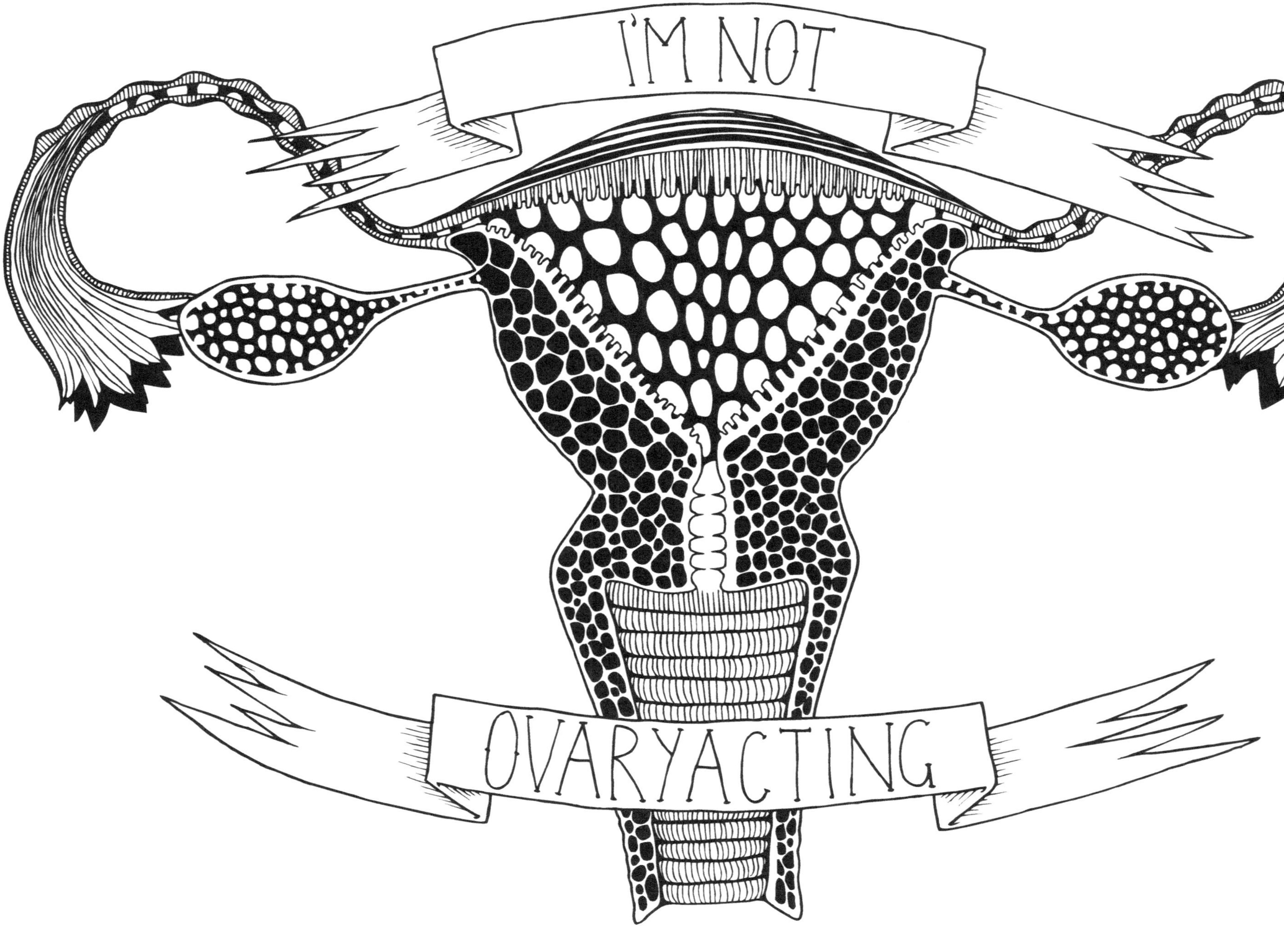
I'M NOT
OVARYACTING

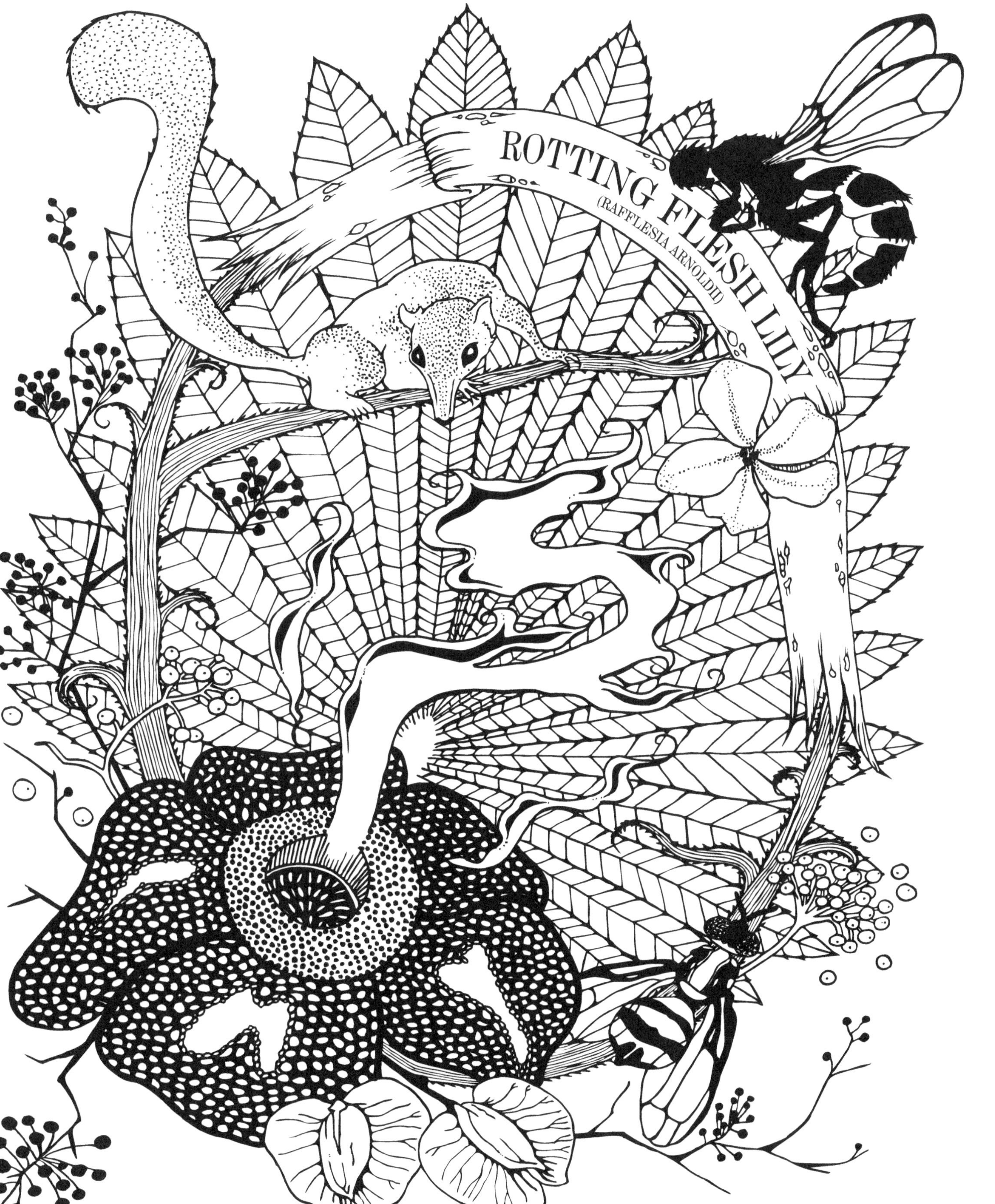
ROTTING FLESH LILY
(RAFFLESIA ARNOLDII)

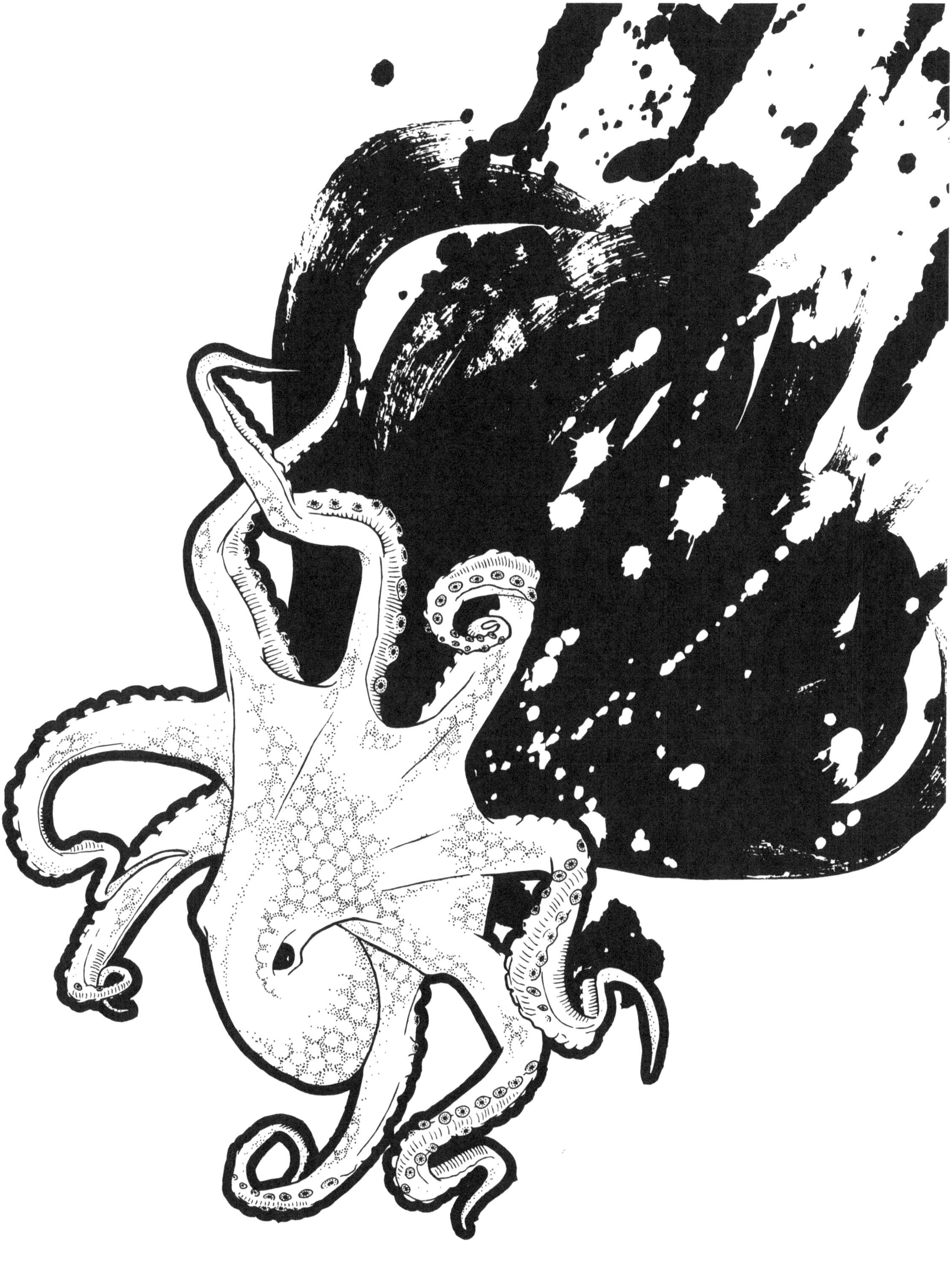

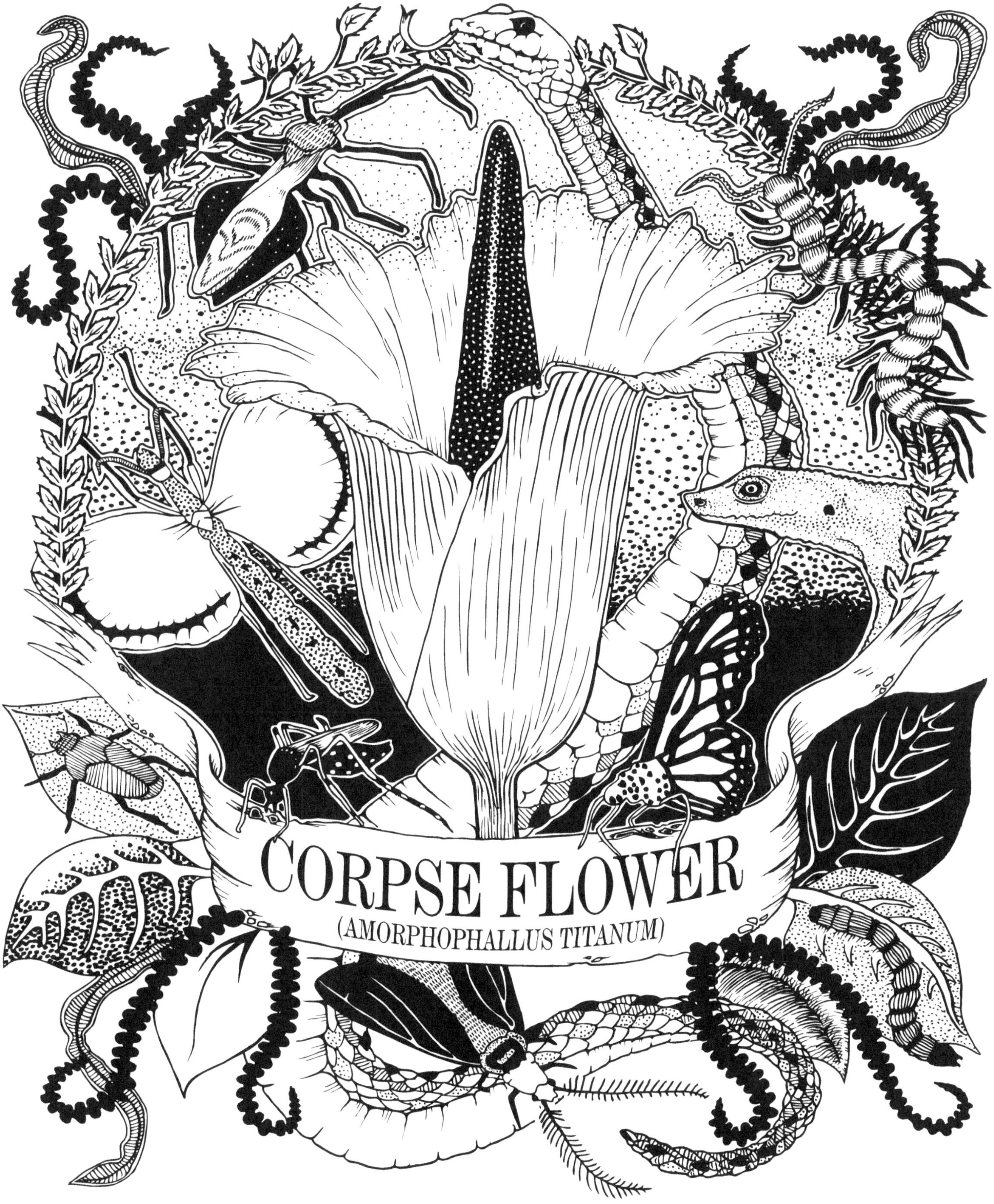
CORPSE FLOWER
(AMORPHOPHALLUS TITANUM)

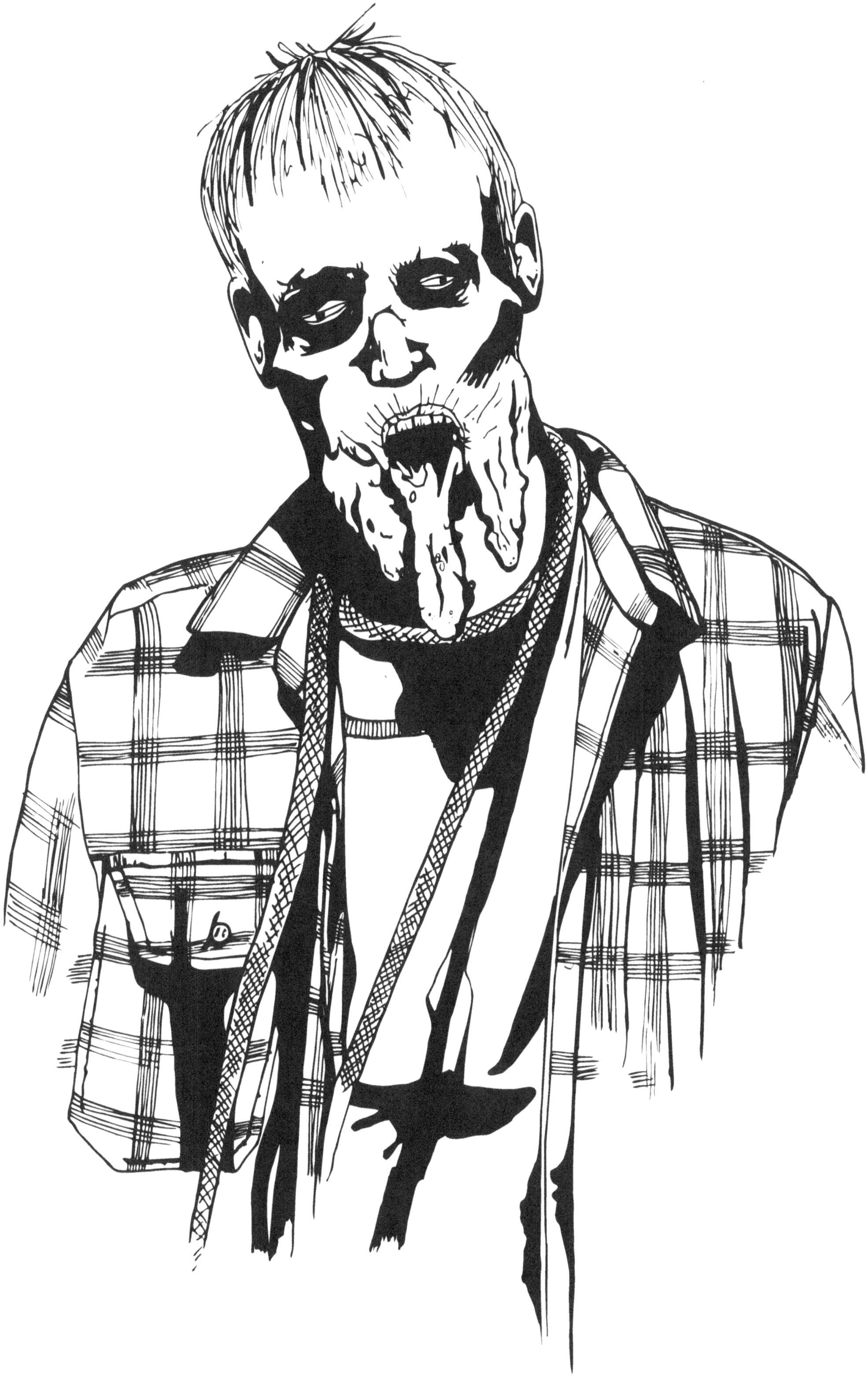

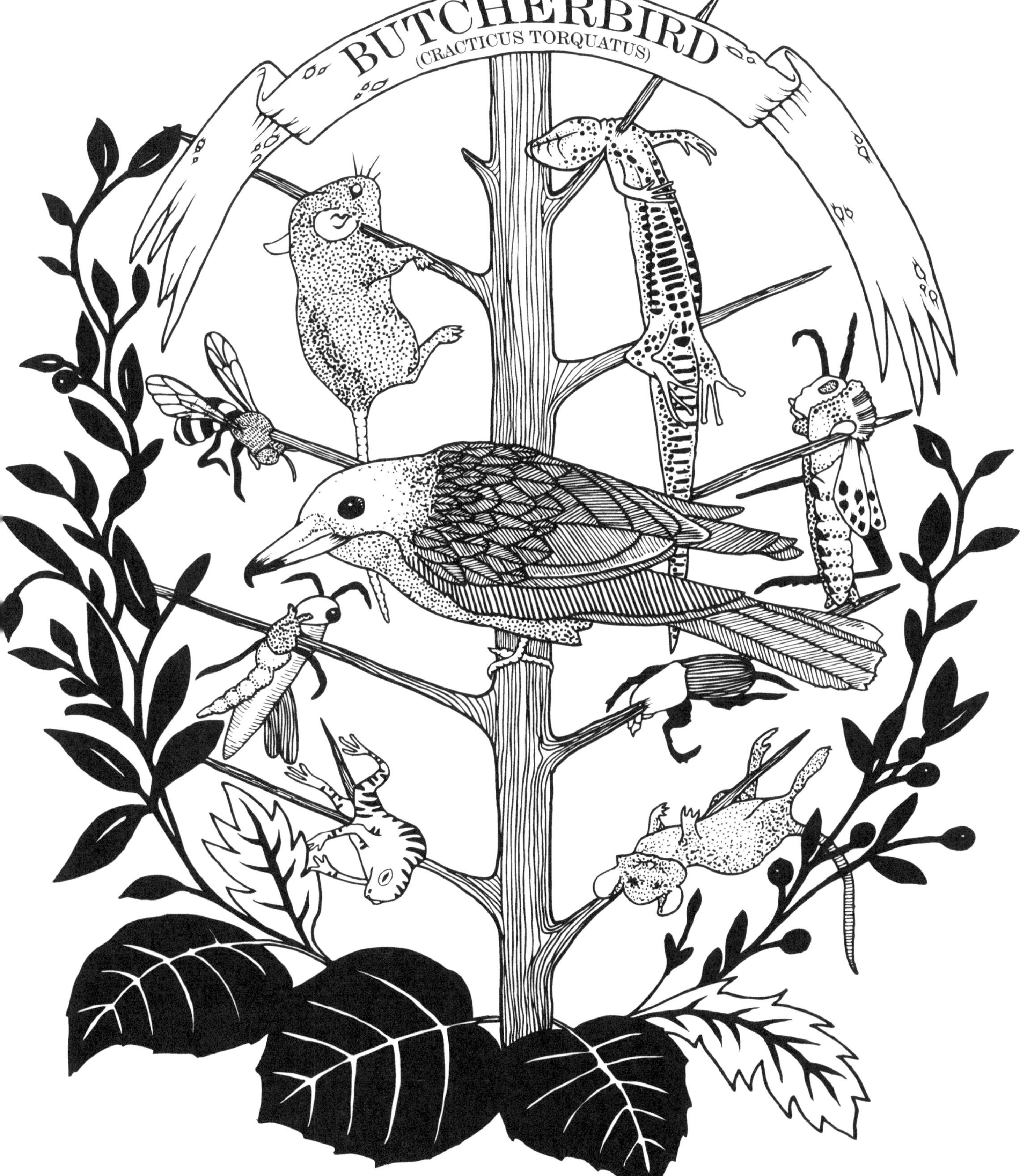
BUTCHERBIRD
(CRACTICUS TORQUATUS)

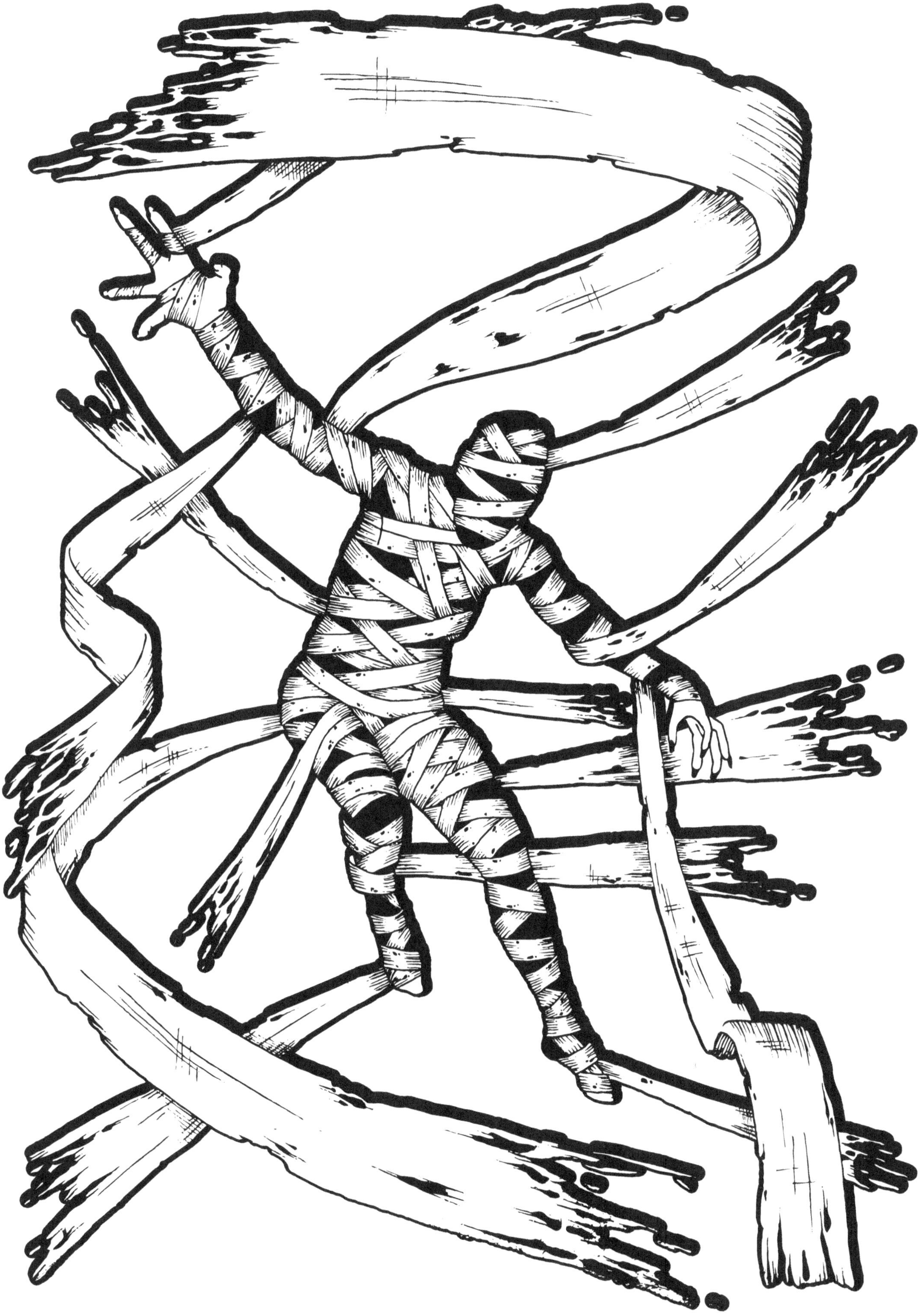

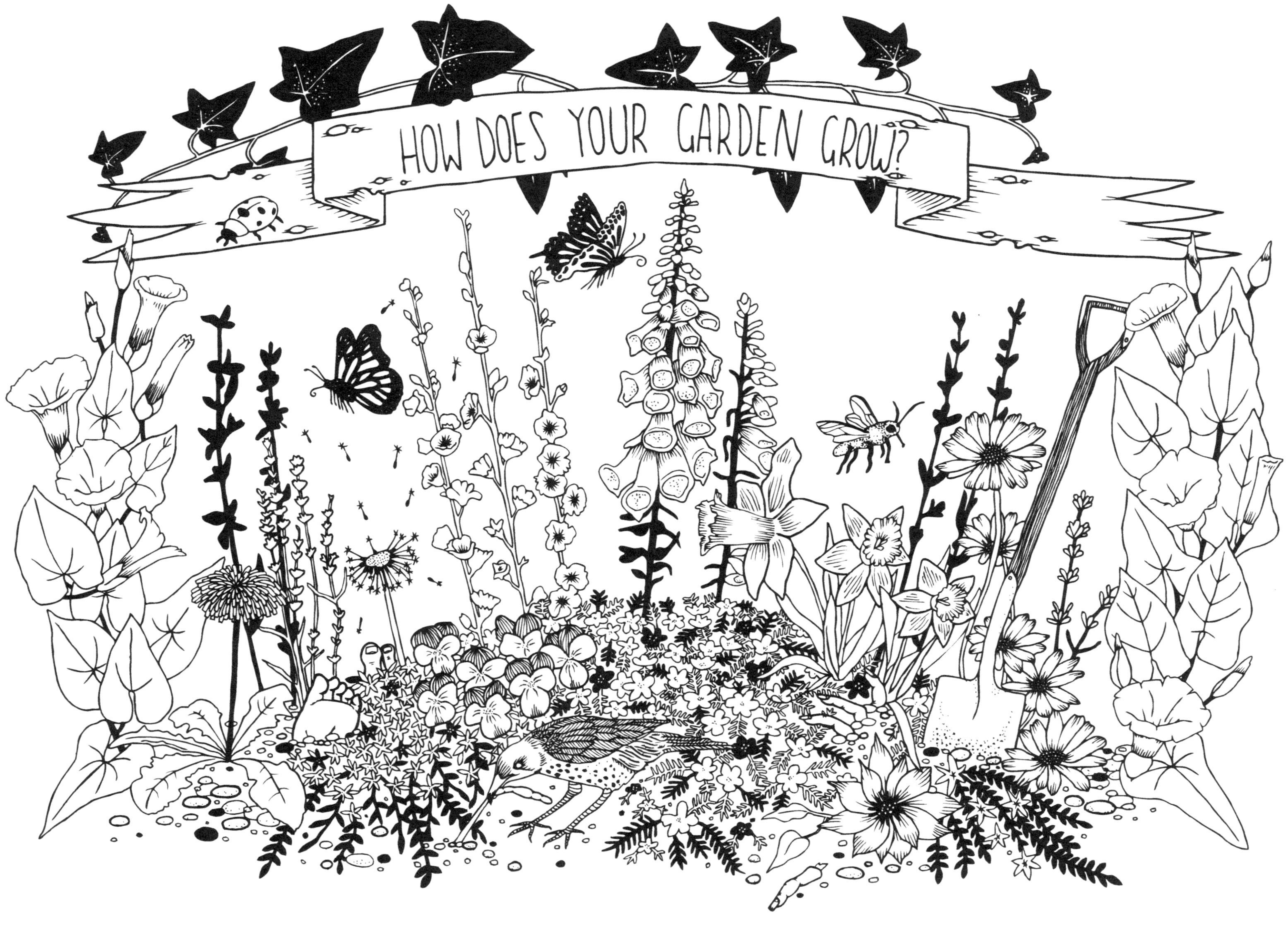
HOW DOES YOUR GARDEN GROW?

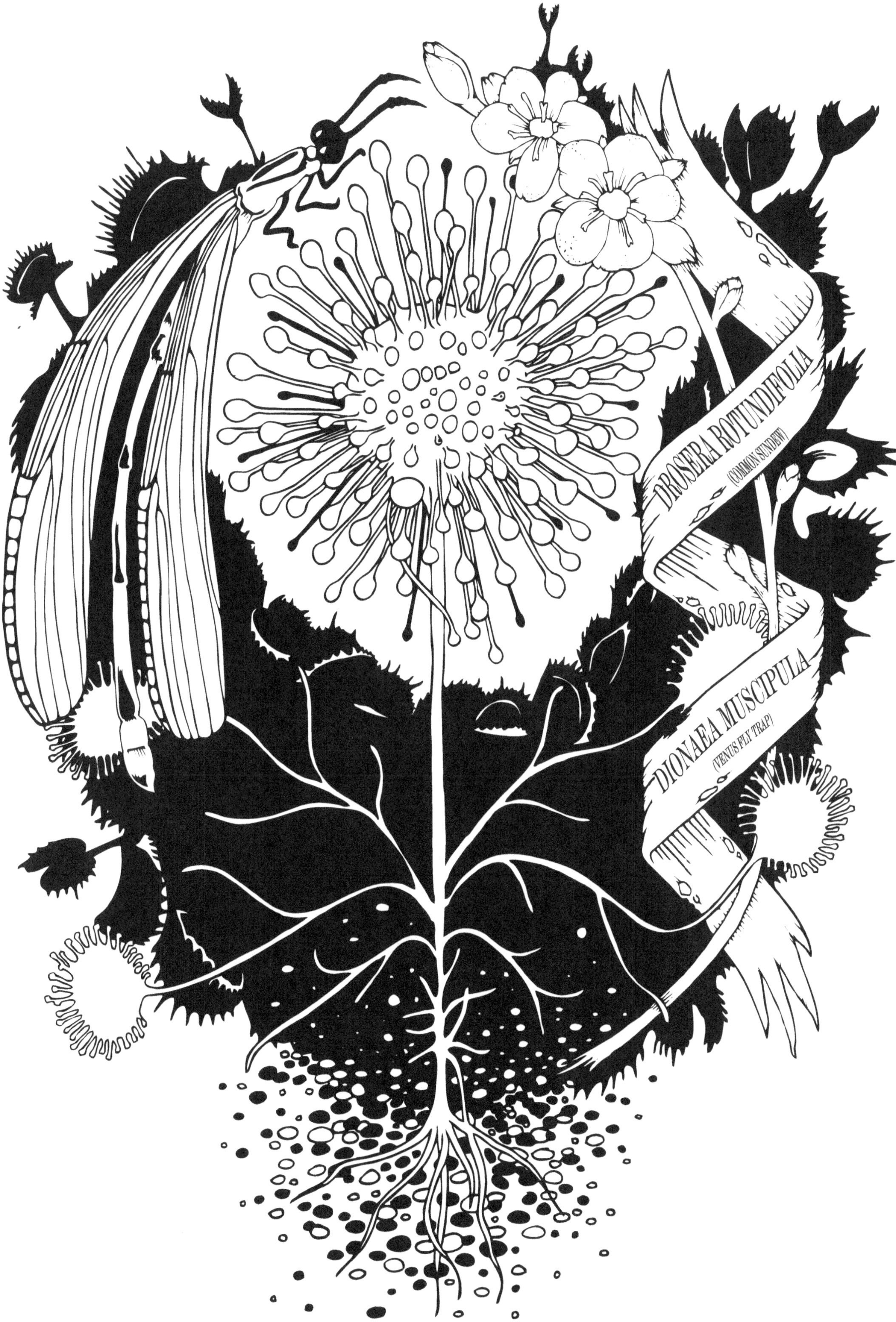
DROSERA ROTUNDIFOLIA
(COMMON SUNDEW)
DIONAEA MUSCIPULA
(VENUS FLY TRAP)

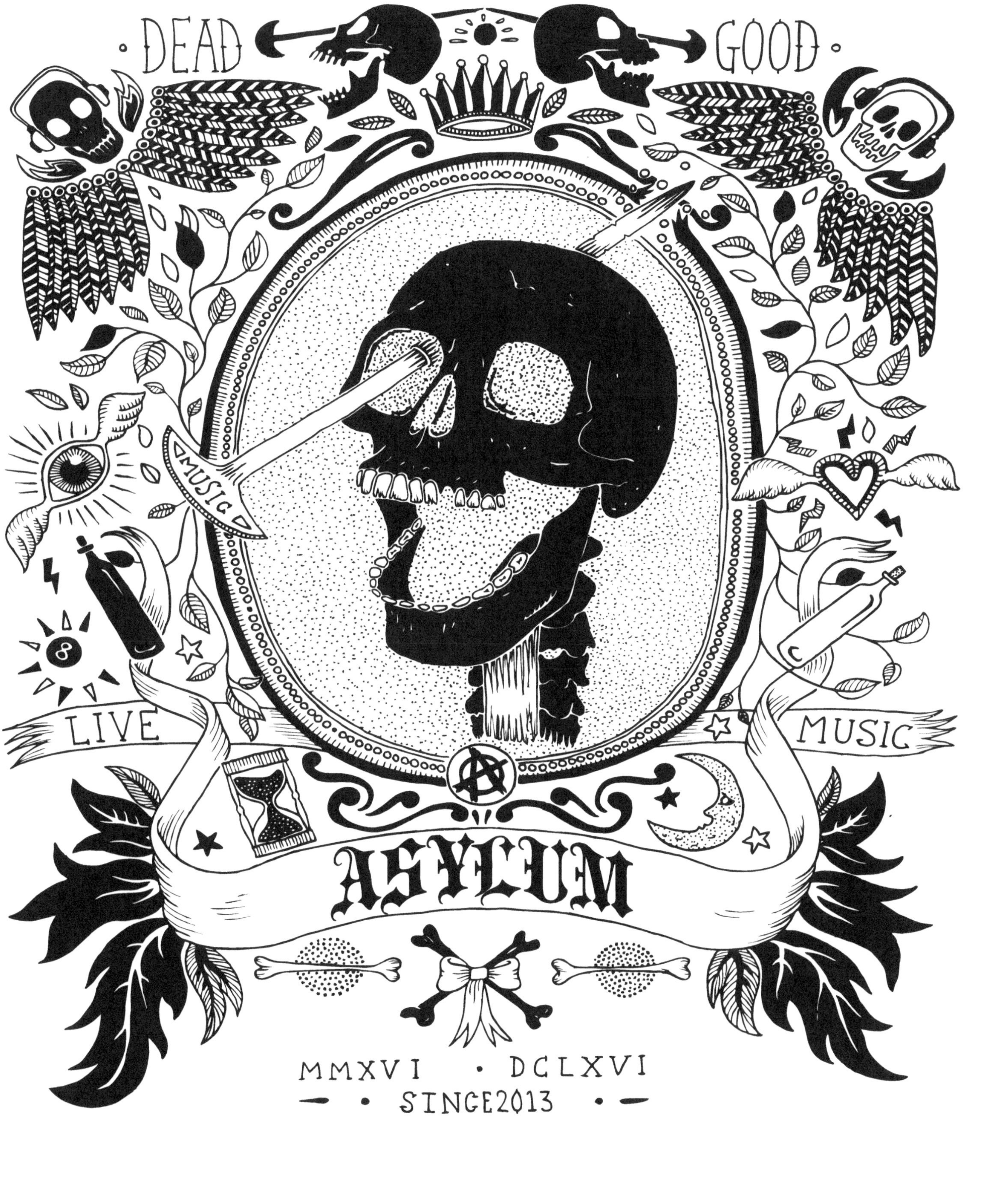
DEAD
GOOD
MUSIC
LIVE
MUSIC
ASYLUM
MMXVI • DCLXVI
• SINCE2013 •

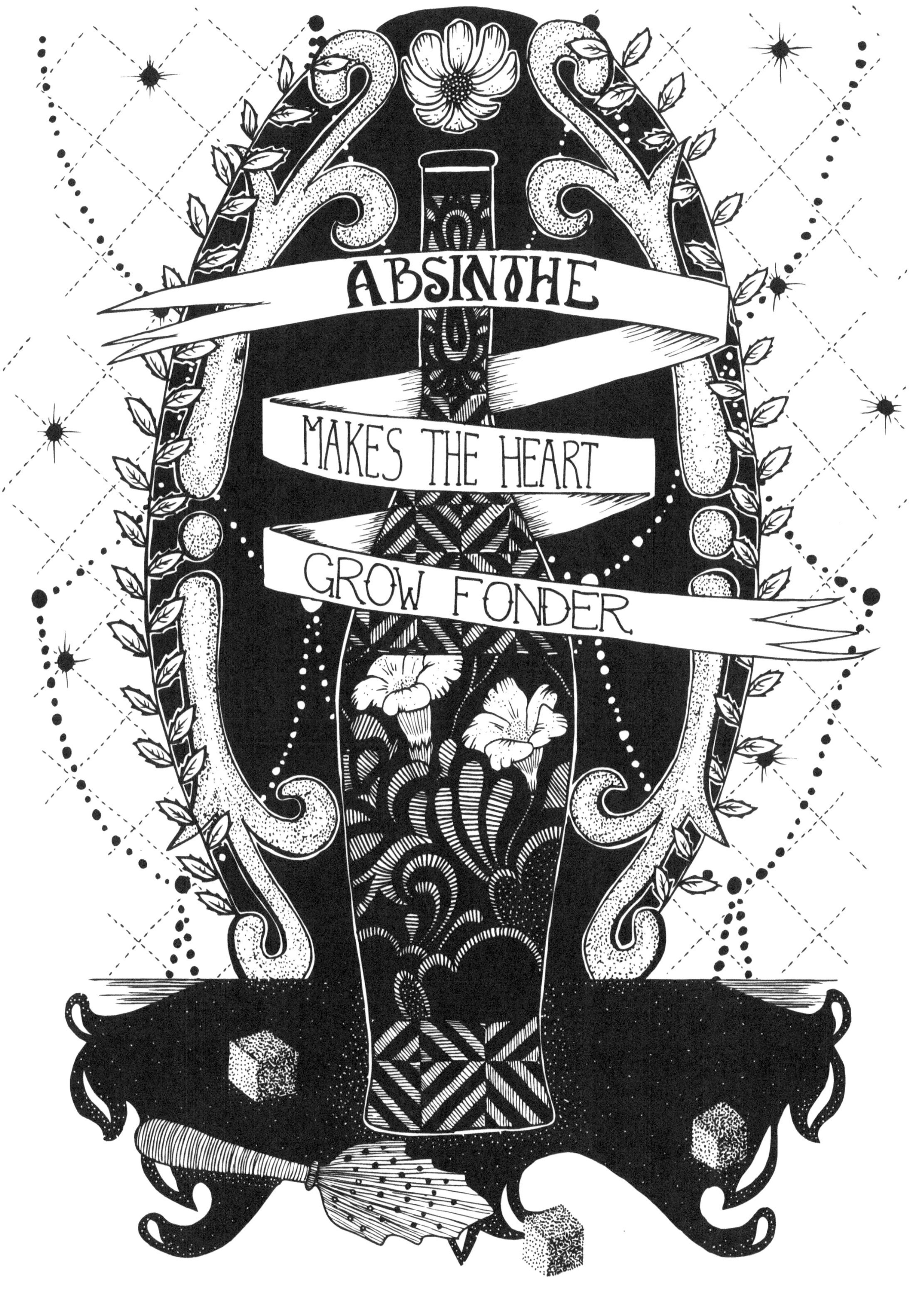
ABSINTHE
MAKES THE HEART
GROW FONDER.

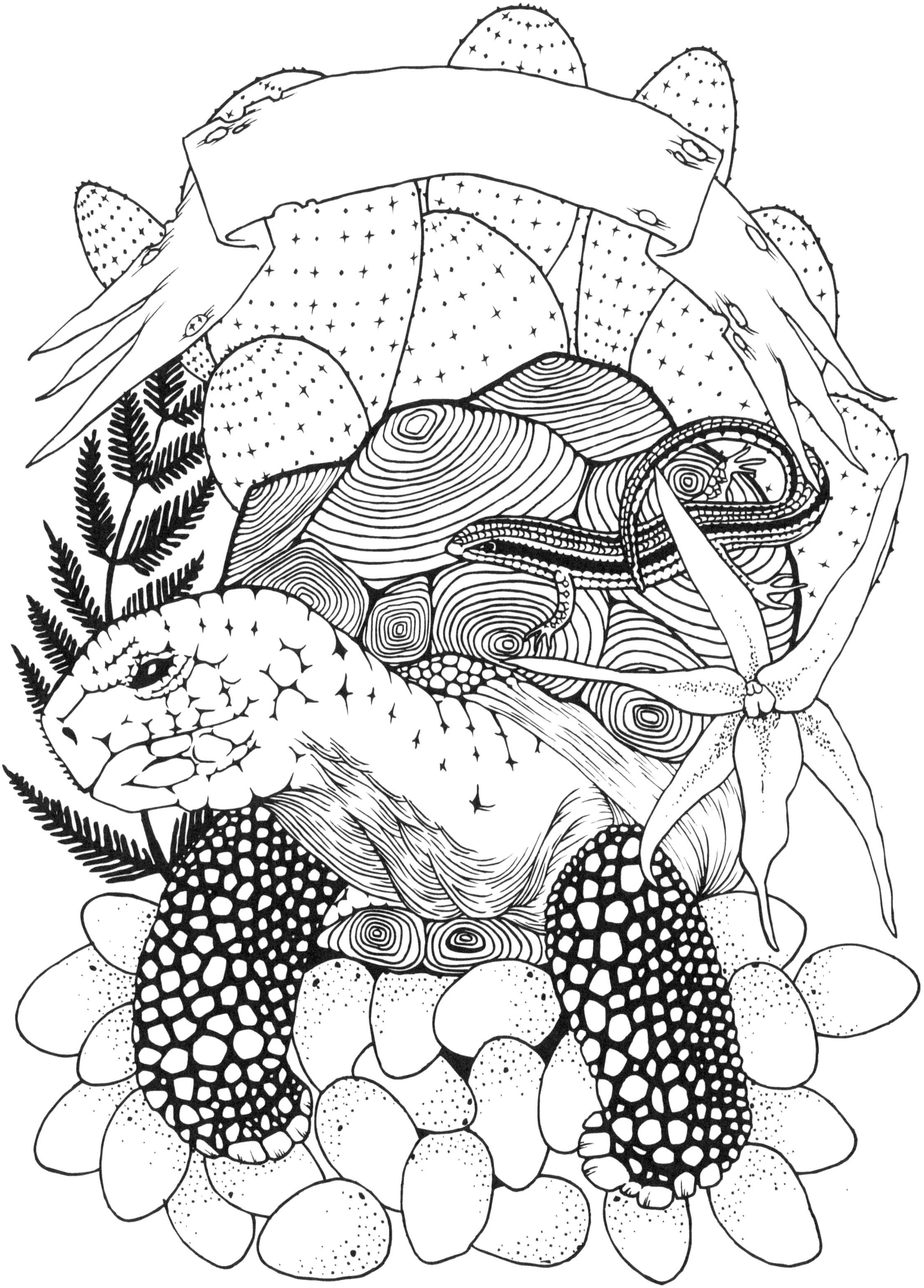

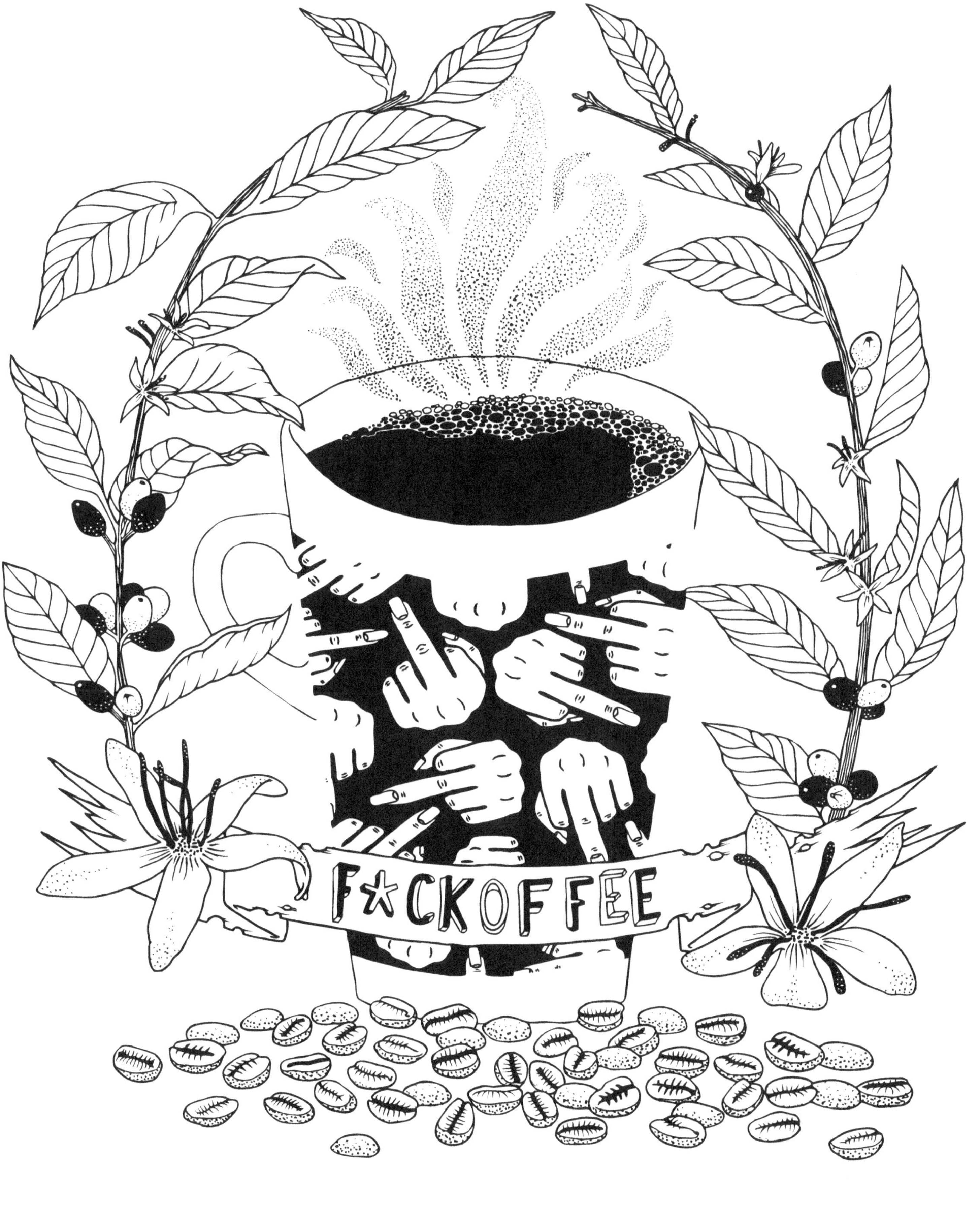
F★CKOFFEE

www.ingramcontent.com/pod-product-compliance
Lightning Source LLC
Chambersburg PA
CBHW081134180526
45170CB00008B/3107
* 9 7 8 1 5 4 6 5 9 4 2 2 2 *